BASIL

BASIL

Katharine Rauk

To Thor —
Katie

Black Lawrence Press

Black Lawrence Press
www.blacklawrence.com

Executive Editor: Diane Goettel
Book Design: Steven Seighman

Cover photograph: *Spruce Girls* by Vern C. Gorst
used with permission of the University of Washington Libraries, Special Collections Division

Text copyright © 2011 Katharine Rauk

All rights reserved. Except for brief quotations in critical articles or reviews, no part of this book may be reproduced in any manner without prior written permission from the publisher:

Black Lawrence Press
115 Center Ave
Aspinwall, PA 15215
U.S.A.

Published 2011 by Black Lawrence Press, an imprint of Dzanc Books

ISBN: 978-0-9826364-5-9

First edition 2011

Printed in the United States

CONTENTS

- 7   Fuse
- 8   The Rapture
- 9   An Assembly of Lit Things
- 10   Self-Portrait with Monkey
- 11   Blood Orange
- 12   Heartbone (I)
- 13   Circumference of the Heartbone
- 14   Heartbone (II)
- 15   Basil
- 16   After Cooking with Turmeric
- 17   Wrecked
- 18   January
- 19   What She Knows
- 20   The Average Person Swallows Four Spiders Per Year While Sleeping
- 21   An Incomplete Guide to North American Toads
- 22   The Ant
- 23   Vignette
- 24   In the End Won't Death Be an Endless Kitchen?
- 25   Suicide Rates Spike Near High-Voltage Power Lines
- 26   How Many Weeks Are in a Day and How Many Years in a Month?
- 27   The Threshing Floor
- 28   The First Goose
- 29   Fever
- 30   Untitled (Le Carte Géographique), 2009
- 31   She Was Born in a Cedar Box

Fuse

She would have an affair with a man named Ulf.
He would eat toasted cheese sandwiches.
He would have square hands.
He would keep a clock on his mantel
which he would wind every noon with a small bronze key.
His refrigerator would contain a compartment for hard-boiled eggs
which she would always keep full.
He would live on an island in the North Sea
which would be accessible by boat every two Thursdays,
so he would not get the newspaper, and she would not
have to read about the Democratic primaries
or Reem Riashi, mother-of-two, first female
suicide bomber for Hamas. She would not be bothered
by those days when the sun never set
but squat interminably on the horizon instead.
And when they would make love,
the ragged edges of the sea would be sealed from sight
by the four sides of the window frame
so she wouldn't hear the squalling
of seabirds that scrawled along the shore
and when Ulf, who would smell faintly of chamomile,
would come, she would come too
and she would be a seabird coasting the wind, no
she would be a jewel of salt, no
she would be a herring among a thousand herrings,
a gleam among a thousand silver shifts, no
she would be the sea, not
its heaves or its hurling but
she would be a shush of foam against the sand,
the sigh of froth and spume, no
she would be the hiss
of a fuse lit and burning, she would explode
like sparks, and would never need to look back
finally, like Reem Riashi would never look back.

The Rapture

> *For you yourselves know perfectly that the day of the Lord*
> *so cometh as a thief in the night.*
> I Thessalonians 5:2

She was ripe
for the plot. Wrapped
in a silk robe, she pleaded
for capture, even a lick
of slim wrath. Roped
to her bedposts—her sleeves
ripped and her wrists
slightly scraped—she
pretended to wait
for the cops (or the one
in a cape). She sham
fainted. She feigned
corpse. Fed up but not
stuffed, she sacked
scripture on her knees
looking for hymns
of seizure. For him
she hummed, trimmed
lamps in the unmanned
mansion of her mind.
Where was the suitor
who would sate her,
who would break her
from this horizontal
life? Who would suture
this body that waited
for rupture?

An Assembly of Lit Things

My boyfriend worked the night shift. I got bored. One Thursday I reached up to change the burnt out light in the back of my classroom & a 60 watt Lumalux Double Life dropped into my palm like an overripe pear. That's when I decided to dedicate myself to light bulb collection. I roamed the hallways of Shortridge Middle School after hours, poking into empty rooms to scavenge for Bulbrite Standbys, Slimline Satin Spunlights, & any incandescent globe. The night janitor knew what I wanted. He'd save specimens for me in his back office, slipping me fluorescent torpedoes, instant starts, & once, a whole boxful of Neptune standard screws. *Why light bulbs?* you might ask. When I spread them over my sheets, I see a flock of soap bubbles fleeing south. Sometimes the wispy filaments become a fleet of miniature ships all sailing to countless horizons inside the same bright bottle of glass.

Self-Portrait with Monkey

My lover says my eyebrows trace
a hummingbird's outstretched wings. That's why
distance sits on my forehead, why
my eyes sail away. But

you're the one
with the wandering eye, baby. That's why
I keep my pet monkey on a string.
And you, my husband, my lover

of sisters, my loaner of hearts,
I can't hold you
nowhere and noways. That's why
my womb keeps

erasing itself. Why I
cherish my monkey's caress. That's why
I've learned to grow
my own moustache and learned

to eat those sugar skulls I make.
Learned you belong to yourself. That's why
you're my husband. My baby. My
necklace of bones.

for Frida Kahlo

Blood Orange

Slice: swollen flesh
brims red.

Is this a fruit,
a wound, a lover?

I ate. We never know
what we'll do

when the body
moves of its own

knowing: my lips
suddenly opening

sectioned windows
soaked in rubied light.

Heartbone (I)

"I've never met a pie I didn't like," he mused, scraping the
jawed edge of his car key between his two front teeth to extract
a raspberry seed that had lodged there. He fixed the seed
on the tip of his index finger, turning it this way and that so
it glistened in the afternoon light until he wiped it into the
furrows of his corduroy pants. But the seed remained in the
pocket behind Chloe's eyes. She held it there, saw it sprout

> noiseless furred legs,
> saw it delve into moist soil
> where it belonged. Yes,
> she saw it, this pregnant clock,
> this hearthstone lost
> in the double-dark, a juice pouch,
> a heartbone dreaming of night and red
> patent leather shoes, the blood beat
> of has-been and will-be and now—"You

know what I'm saying?" he repeated a third time, pushing
himself back from the table.

Circumference of the Heartbone

The moon was outside
my body.

The potatoes slept beneath
my feet: pale

dirt pearls, their bellies
swollen

with buried light. As for
the heartbone

no one knows whether it is
sleeping.

If it's waiting or growing
and where.

What do I want from the moon?
Confirmation

of circumference: even if you can't
see her all at once

she's still there.

Heartbone (II)

My nub, my sweetness, my buried
bruise. My blue note and knotted
fruit stone, my blood knocking at the edge
of known. Made of root bits and flesh
snips, snarls of hair that won't let
loose. Made of loss, made of juice,
made of mud and mud and mud
that sings. Heartbone—dearest
fiend, my honeyed shard, my tiny
swollen warp—when I find you
will I be found or not found?

Basil

In India, they place me in the mouths
of the dying

to ensure swift passage to God.
I taste sharp: the distance

between earth and stars,
wind keening along fence posts

containing a garden,
nights stung by rain.

You, who don't know
your own face

even as you bury it
in your hands,

who bruise me
between your fingertips

but have never swallowed me
whole: eat

so you can speak
to God of such things.

After Cooking with Turmeric

My stained fingertips trace
your lips, the line
of your nose, one eyebrow
after another. Now
we are opening
vaulted windows
to a sunlight of bees,
a thousand burnished
throats. Now we are smudged
with Gobi sand, its taste
for heat. Now we smell
of freshly split wood,
that splintered moment
when lightning licks open
the heart of a tree.

Wrecked

        White pillows tossed
like so much foam,
              a headboard thrashed
        into cedar shards—
each one etched by the squiggled hallways
             beetles eat into wood
        like the twists of a difficult sonata
or the channels inside a woman's body
              where even music gets lost—
        fish scales littering the sand
to assemble a ruin
             of stained glass.

January

She saw how the trees' shadows lay down
with the shadows already collected
inside each footprint in the snow—which
wasn't white, exactly,
but a color that leaned like the trees'
shadows leaned (the trees unbalanced
by the sun's thinning glow)—the snow,
was it blue? no, the color of afterthought,
maybe, of imitated light—

and here she wavered, but not the shadows
(those sharp replies), not the bristling
wreckage of leaves that breached
the snow. Not the footprints that walked away.

What She Knows

The woman is inhabited
by a field swept with snow. Which she keeps
sweeping. The rhythm is satisfactory
because it is all she knows.

Each stroke soughs in a different tone:

a scythe threshing hay—
        stones lashed by sea—
                a comb pulling swiftly through hair—

wind in a stairwell—
        curtains tearing—
                a whetstone scraped by a knife—

And on nights without wind
        in a dark without hands
                she hears

                        Yes?   *Yes?*   *Yes?*

The Average Person Swallows Four Spiders Per Year While Sleeping

The spider descends into her abdominal cavity like a spelunker hitched to a nylon zipline. But he prefers to think of himself as a wooden bucket lowered into a well—what long-drowned wish will he retrieve? He's got work to do. He starts with the spleen: his three spinnerets cast girdles of silk around that obsolete seat of emotion (mostly melancholy) until it's wound tight as Spring in a seed. The liver, double-lobed vessel of bile, is the daunting next task. This organ's battle-scarred and ornery, barnacles clinging to its belly like the crusty memories of good days gone bad. Luckily this is one persistent spider. He slings skeins of silk around the liver until it's trussed up like a baleen about to be boarded by Ahab's crew: blubber to be stripped for candles soon to light late-night missives blotted with tears, whalebone slated for corset stays like so many cages of teeth. The spider wraps the gallbladder, the duodenum, the ascending colon, then stops to glance around. It's as if he's in a country manor abandoned by nobility, the last loyal butler having draped the furniture in shrouds. Only the stomach's left to be beribboned, which he soon does. Let's see what she hungers for now...

That night she dreams of the Forbidden City. Behind its nine walls, inside one of its 9,999 rooms, a servant is forced to lie flat on his back upon a wooden board. The ceremony begins: someone dips a band of white silk in a basin and winds it about his feet. Another binds his hands. Then his body is swathed in strip after strip of soaked silk as if his existence were an open wound. Soon he will be cocooned for his crime: coveting the empress' lips, which he covered with his own. You'd think he'd know better than to mess with Golden Orb Weaver, dowager with the defiantly big feet who, like a female spider, relishes the execution of mates. Finally even the servant's mouth is swaddled in wet silk (spun to a warp of 2,000 threads) and he swills his own breaths and bellows, drowning on the Inner Court's sand. The palace eunuchs scuttle away through the tangled corridors, their testicles cloistered in small cloth sacks.

Did you know spiders are able to digest their own silk? A spider can skim down a single gossamer strand, which it will swallow on the way back up. That's what this one did.

An Incomplete Guide to North American Toads

Physical Appearance

Not to be confused with frogs,
which are smooth as the skin on a young boy's knuckles,
toads are dry, knobbled, stubby, and squat.
They are blotched, olive, rusted, green.
The skin of the female toad is rougher than the male's
and more often mottled with bumps.

The Mating Call

Toads buzz, or trill, or spin high-pitched whistles,
or grunt like crows in complaint.
The Southwestern Woodhouse Toad screams
like a nail wrenched from wood.
Fowler's Toad sings with one voice in Little Rock
and another in the Blue Ridge Mountains.

The Mating Silence

Most females are mute.
They do not have
dark throat sacks that swell.

What Some Women Know

La Llorona wades through nights
wailing. She is the White Woman
who weeps toads
the muddy green of graves,
and she drags a river behind her
in which her children have drowned.
The villagers bolt the latches when they hear her through their windows,
except for the grandmothers who have ruined much bread
and the young women who are learning to listen.

"Amphibios" or "Double Life"

Horned sickles hook on the hind legs of the Spadefoot
for burrowing underground.
She is a stubborn root that out-sits death
until puddles summon
and she releases her eggs like strands of black pearls.

What to Look Out For

Toads have poison glands behind their eyes.

What to Look For

When Aztecs look at the moon
they see a toad swallowing a knife.
When this moon spits
light onto the fields, the corn stalks
cast shadows like blades.

Miscellaneous

The Oak Toad is the size of an eyeball
that has seen the heart of the swamp.
You could hold this toad in your palm.
It might have once belonged
inside your body
and has now come out to tell you
what secrets it knows.

The Ant

"It might be a bullet ant," Jack reported at dinner. "The sting of the bullet ant rates the highest of any ant species on the Schmidt Pain Index." Jack was well-informed about such subjects. Maude admired the glossiness of the ant's head, the way he shivered the serrated spurs that graced the end of each one of his six legs when she tenderly stroked his scape. She imagined unsnapping his polished carapace, swinging open his two sides to find interlocking chambers intricate as clockwork, each one ticking like a newborn violin. The room took on the luster of well-worn wooden spoons. The hour of clouds had begun. Outside the window, a telephone line stretched across the backyard, a single uncut string.

Vignette

She was wishing for a child
so she tied a cucumber to her waist.

Cucumber vines crept beyond
the edges of the garden plot
like sticky fingers swiping from the sweet jar.

A cucumber, even one
that's set in the sun all afternoon,
holds cold
like a white bite of moon:
what can't be
tied down.

In the End
Won't Death Be an Endless Kitchen?

from Pablo Neruda's Book of Questions

If we are the leftovers
from Monday's primordial soup, does that mean
Sunday we go back into the pot,
boiled at a temperature befitting
our unique recipe of sin? Or, like a carrot,
will our skin be stripped into slick ringlets and tossed
to the bottom of a porcelain sink?
Will we suffer
chokes of steam, the steely gaze
of cleavers, a garlic press of sinister size?

Or does it mean that in death
we are full
of what we have been
fed? Or is no one ever
full, even in death? Beats me.
I'm like the sea,
who is never full, no matter how many
rivers and rains she swallows,
for even when her belly strains against the seam of shore
she still finds room for dinghies, docks, and
forgotten tambourines, for trails the gulls disclose
in air, for clutters of spring-storm twigs, and
for chipped bottles, all their jagged edges
begging for smooth.

Suicide Rates Spike Near High-Voltage Power Lines

She knew why: all those unseen ions shivering through the air. She could feel them. And she could hear them too, which was lucky because she knew the metal switch box outside her apartment window, high up and to the east, was the very voice box of God. Always—but especially in the evenings when darkness thickened and the city lit up like a swarm of krill—she felt God's voice thrum around the rims of teacups, pulse along the floorboards' crease. She waited in the bedroom, on top of the sheets. She felt

>God's voice
>sizzle in her teeth, she felt
>God's voice surge
>down the wire
>of her spine, and
>God's voice gather
>in the satellite
>saucers of her knees until
>every cell became
>current, until the soft
>loaf of her flesh became
>one taut string, became
>sound singed to quick, became
>a syllable strung over rooftops
>at silverpitch—

How Many Weeks Are in a Day and How Many Years in a Month?

from Pablo Neruda's Book of Questions

How many hours in a peach
that swallows light
like a woman with her secret
windows, each pain a glass
which opens onto orchards
sown with how many
bites of time?
How many minutes in the room
where rain is born
with her sudden bouquet of hands
which flattens furrows
hewn in foreheads
and presses how many
thumbprints in the grass?
How many seconds in a question
seeded in the dirt
as when the peach's ribbed pit asks
shall I come?
and its tender flesh asks
shall I go?

The Threshing Floor

Father says to flail the wheat.
I tread the heaps of grain
with my bare feet,
thinking of the horses trotting round
and round the riding ring.
The grass is flat there.
Sometimes it's best to lie down.
The bits flare in the horses' mouths.
Their flanks are river-muscles
that never stop surging.

Father says to winnow
the wheat upon the wind.
I fling the loosened grain above my head
and the wind takes what it will.
It also takes
the birds. They are lost
to my small eyes, but their wings,
which open and close
and open again, are not lost
to the sky which bears them.

Father says to burn the chaff.
I know he means to separate
the good parts from the bad.
But finished loaves of bread,
when thumped, sound hollow. Besides,
you cannot burn the chaff that burns itself
like morning mist that bakes away in sun.
Or the chaff that, like smoke,
can slip through threshold cracks.

The First Goose

The father leans against the iron
               railing of the bridge,
     hands tucked into his down vest while
the girl, stalled, stares at
              the goose that lurches down the wooden planks
     towards her. The father sees the goose
but not the chilling curvature
              of its neck, a question mark
     hooking the air. Not
the feathers snaggled by wind, not
              the feet blooming dark
     stains on the boards of the bridge, not
the head like the hammer
              of a piano key about to fall. The girl,
     eyes now fisted shut, stands
at the river's weed-clotted edge
              beneath one elm
     that hoards the light,
and all around the girl (tender
              spindle of green) hums
     the betrayal of leaves, hums
                  the pitched sky.

Fever

A heron sits on her chest.
        His wet-wracked
body stinks of marsh—black
        muck, massed leaves, the dank
of the buried unearthed—
        which coats her throat but
she can't cough. Still
        the heron weights her chest
with his scaly legs
        upon which everything is balanced—

Untitled (Le Carte Géographique), 2009

a box after Joseph Cornell

The usual accoutrements: a miniature metronome, a pinch of sand, a broken tuning fork. Six pearl beads strung with one fleck of bone. A silk tulip dyed blue. Cork-stopped bottle furnished with golden filaments and crumpled tulle. A cutout of Le Carte Géographique de la Lune. But the centerpiece is an agate plucked from Lake Erie's northern shore. Since its hues and half-shades are most brilliant while stunned underwater, the stone has been placed in a glass dish that collects rain from a bit of plastic tubing snipped from an aquarium filter that protrudes from the roof of the box. During dry spells, an attendant has been hired to fill its spout with dew. She keeps bouquets of thistle in her apron pockets, an iron nail tucked behind one ear. Jerry-rigged to the bony hump on her back are two wings fashioned from the tail feathers of an ancient Scarlet Macaw once trained to rasp, "Who's there? Who's there?"

She Was Born in a Cedar Box

and is kept there
inside the smell of lakeshore, the one
which begins in April, the one
where her parents walked
together but now no longer walk, where
the grass speaks names
and no one waits
and someone squeezes an accordion
which brims the air with oranges
and breathes out gusts of black roosters
and builds stairwells of up and down and even
sideways, for the sound underneath is the sound
of wind sawing in the trees
and sanded planks set in place
and a cedar box snapped shut so its sweet scents
open in the darkness in which
days do not begin
but are always beginning to end.

Acknowledgements

Grateful acknowledgment is made to the editors of the following journals in which some of these poems first appeared, sometimes in different forms.

Slipstream: "Fuse" (originally titled "Looking Ahead") and "The Average Person Swallows Four Spiders per Year While Sleeping"

The Spoon River Poetry Review: "The Rapture" and "Suicide Rates Spike near High-Voltage Power Lines"

Wild Apples: "Basil," "After Cooking with Turmeric," and "Blood Orange"

Zone 3: "January" and "She Was Born in a Cedar Box"

Katharine Rauk earned a M.A. in Humanities from the University of Chicago and a M.F.A. in poetry from the Bennington Writing Seminars. She has poems published or forthcoming in many national literary journals such as *Harvard Review*, *Georgetown Review*, *Cream City Review*, *Zone 3*, and others, and she is an assistant editor of *Rowboat: Poetry in Translation*. She lives and teaches in Minneapolis.